F

Being a Plant

BEING

A PLANT

Laurence Pringle

ILLUSTRATIONS BY

ROBIN BRICKMAN

Thomas Y. Crowell

New York

*The author wishes to thank Dr. Richard Klein,
Professor of Botany, University of Vermont, for reading the
manuscript of this book and helping to improve its accuracy.*

BEING A PLANT

Text copyright © 1983 by Laurence Pringle
Illustrations copyright © 1983 by Robin Brickman
For information address
Thomas Y. Crowell Junior Books, 10 East 53rd Street,
New York, N.Y. 10022. Published simultaneously in
Canada by Fitzhenry & Whiteside Limited, Toronto.
Designed by Constance Fogler
1 2 3 4 5 6 7 8 9 10
First Edition

Library of Congress Cataloging in Publication Data
Pringle, Laurence P.
    Being a plant.

    Includes: bibliography, p.
    Includes: index, p.
    Summary: This examination of plants includes
a discussion of their internal structure, their
ability to make their own food, their adapt-
ability, and their complex relationship with
other living things.
    1. Plants—Juvenile literature. [1. Plants]
I. Brickman, Robin, ill.   II. Title
QK49.P74 1983   581   82-45915
ISBN 0-690-04346-5
ISBN 0-690-04347-3 (lib. bdg.)

Contents

Being a Plant

CHAPTER ONE

Plants Are Like and Unlike Animals

In his diary, the great English scientist Charles Darwin once jotted down the reminder "Prove plants like animals." Although Darwin did not pursue this idea, other scientists have since discovered that plants are, indeed, similar to animals in many ways.

Both plants and animals take in gases, water, and minerals. They reproduce and react to changing conditions in their surroundings. The basic building blocks of both plants and animals are cells, some of which produce chemicals that help regulate growth and activity. At the microscopic level, the structure and the chemistry of plants and animals are much alike.

Several years ago, some people claimed that they had found yet another similarity between plants and animals.

(3)

They said that plants respond to human emotions, thoughts, and prayers, and that one plant can communicate with another.

These claims, however appealing, have proved untrue. Plants lack the nervous system of animals. There is no evidence that plants have feelings. In their own way, however, plants are just as remarkable as animals. In fact, as we learn more about them, it becomes clear that plants have abilities and adaptations that are as fascinating as any in nature.

When people first began to study the variety of life on earth, they separated organisms into two groups—animals and plants. In this classification, plants range in size from 90-meter (300-foot) trees to microscopic one-celled bacteria. They include not only trees, tulips, and other familiar green plants, but also bacteria, brown and red algae, and such fungi as molds and mildews. Some microscopic organisms, however, are not clearly plant or animal, but have characteristics of both. *Euglena*, for example, can make its own food, like a green plant, but has no cell wall and in other ways is more like a microscopic animal. Should we then call it a plantimal? Or is the choice between two kingdoms—plant or animal—too narrow for the great diversity of life on earth?

It is more sensible, some biologists believe, to separate living things into five kingdoms. According to this arrangement, all organisms that are one celled or that form colonies of cells are within either the monera kingdom (bacteria and blue-green algae) or the protista kingdom (other algae, *Euglena*, and protozoans). All multicelled organisms are within either the fungus (molds, mushrooms), plant, or animal kingdom. The plant kingdom alone includes more than 300,000 kinds of green, multicelled organisms. These plants, and especially flowering plants, are the subject of this book.

CELL WALLS

The most obvious difference between plants and animals is that most plants do not move around. They remain fixed in one place for life, a characteristic that certainly affects how they look. Yet such animals as barnacles, corals, and sea anemones are also stationary for most of their lives. So lack of mobility in plants is not as great a distinction as it first appears to be.

A more significant difference between plants and animals is in the structure of their cells. Both plant and animal cells are surrounded by living membranes, but only

(5)

plant cells have walls. The wall of a young plant cell is very thin and elastic. When a cell reaches its full size, its wall has several layers and is more rigid. These layers are made partly of lignin, a chemical compound that gives wood much of its strength; thus, it could be said that plant cells live in wooden boxes. Cell walls help support plants while they live and after they die.

Like animals, plants are made up of many different kinds of cells. Some are specially adapted to pass along liquids. Cells that form the bark of trees or the shells of nuts have extremely tough cell walls. Others, called meristem cells, divide again and again, continually forming new cells. Meristem cells are found at the tips of roots and stems, or wherever growth by cell division occurs. Plants, unlike animals, grow only in certain parts and never truly stop growing.

FOOD MAKING

Leaves are made of several kinds of cells, including those that aid the flow of liquids. A leaf surface has a single layer of epidermal cells that secretes a waxy covering called cuticle. This substance helps reduce water loss from the leaves. Although thickest on the upper surface of the leaf,

(6)

cuticle is transparent, allowing sunshine to pass through to the large, rectangular palisade cells within. Each palisade cell contains about fifty tiny green football-shaped objects called chloroplasts, which contain the green substance chlorophyll. Chlorophyll, more than any other fea-

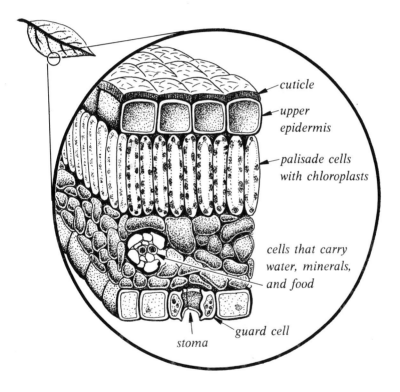

A three-dimensional enlarged view of cells that make up leaves

ture, distinguishes plants from animals because it enables the plant to manufacture food. This process, called photosynthesis ("putting together with light"), uses solar energy to form simple sugars from water and carbon dioxide gas. Later the sugars can be converted to starch, protein, or fat. Thus, photosynthesis changes light energy to food (chemical) energy.

Photosynthesis is the single most important chemical process on earth. It sustains green plants, and as a result, all other living things as well. Both directly and indirectly, green plants generate most of the world's chemical energy. Wood and fossil fuels—coal, oil, and natural gas formed from plants and animals that lived millions of years ago—provide much of our electricity and heat. Green plants are the source of the gasoline we use to power autos and buses. And fresh vegetables, fruits, grains, as well as meat from animals that eat plants, give us the energy to hold a book, turn a page, move our eyes, and to think.

All of this energy originally comes from the sun, and it is available to us only as a result of photosynthesis. People have dreamed of duplicating this process, and biochemists are still trying to unravel its complexities. They know it involves a sequence of chemical changes that takes place in a millionth of a second. They have also discovered that most chlorophyll molecules and certain plant pigments act as antennas, which receive and absorb solar energy, then transmit it to a pair of very special chlorophyll molecules that convert it to chemical energy. When the chemical dynamics of this process are finally understood, people will be much closer to an extraordinary goal, that of converting sunlight directly to chemical energy. Until that goal is achieved, we remain totally dependent on green plants for life.

The chemistry of photosynthesis is just one frontier in botany—the science of studying plants. Botanists are also trying to learn more about how plants grow, reproduce, and adapt to changes in their environments. This book explains some recent findings, and also explores some of the mysteries of the green flowering organisms that continue to intrigue botanists today.

CHAPTER TWO

Moving Water, Food, and Gases

During a drought, a plant's leaves wilt. The entire plant may droop. It is fighting for its life.

Any plant or animal cell soon dies if exposed to air because, in a sense, it is an aquatic organism. In order to survive, it must have water both inside and outside its cell membrane so that various substances can pass through. A plant is a collection of these aquatic cells. Although cuticle, bark, or other material protects this aquatic life somewhat, a plant must continuously absorb and circulate large amounts of water.

A plant has another plumbing problem: providing all cells with food. Not only does every leaf cell need a constant supply of water and minerals from the root system, but every root cell needs a food supply from the leaves. In a large tree, liquids may move 150 meters (500 feet) up or down. A tree's plumbing system—in all its roots, stems, and leaves—may be thousands of miles long.

Water is carried through tracheid and vessel cells, which make up tissue called xylem. Tracheids develop long, thick walls and then die. Through the walls, which are pitted, water passes readily from one cell to another. Vessel cells develop so that they are joined end to end as well as side to side. The end walls dissolve when the cells are fully formed. After the cells die, their joined sidewalls form long, hollow tubes through which water flows easily. Bundles of these water-carrying cells extend throughout plants, from the tips of roots to the uppermost leaves. Strands of tracheids and vessels bring water close to every living cell in a plant.

Sugars, dissolved in water, move through another plumbing system composed of phloem cells. The cells have tiny holes in their end walls—like sieves—which allow the sugary sap to pass through. As long lines of these cells develop, they form sieve tubes. These tubes are living tissue, though their activities seem to be controlled in some way by adjoining cells.

Sieve tubes in plants are the main source of food for aphids and other sap-feeding insects. These insects have

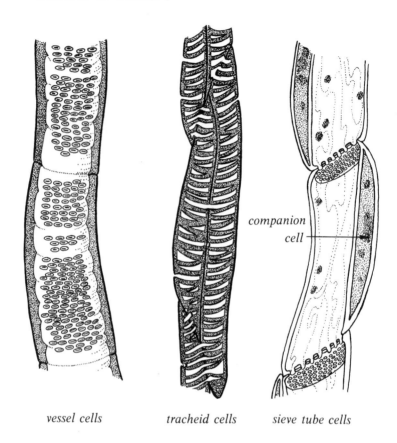

vessel cells   tracheid cells   sieve tube cells

Water moves through vessel and tracheid cells, while food is trans-ported through sieve tubes.

piercing, sucking mouthparts, like delicate hypodermic needles, with which they probe for sieve tubes. A botanist sometimes uses aphids to study the flow and chemistry of plant sap. After an aphid has tapped some sieve tubes of

(12)

a plant, the botanist cuts the insect away from its mouthparts. For several hours the sap continues to flow out of the plant through the mouthparts. It can then be collected and analyzed without harm to the plant.

All together, sieve tubes, tracheids, and vessels make up the liquid-conducting system of plants. It differs from the circulatory system of animals in several ways. In a human, for instance, a muscular heart controls the flow of blood, which carries food and oxygen to cells and takes wastes, including carbon dioxide, from them. Gases are exchanged between blood and air that is brought into and taken out of the body through the lungs. Blood cells make many round trips through the circulatory system.

Plants have two conducting systems—one for water, one for food. Neither carries gases, and neither is powered by a heart. The fluids are not recirculated, and within each system the flow may change direction, depending on the season, the time of day, and other factors.

For a long time, botanists puzzled over how food flows through plants. Sugary sap, they discovered, may move up or down through sieve tubes. Sometimes it moves in opposite directions simultaneously, through adjoining sieve tubes. Sugars always flow from their sources—wherever food is manufactured—to places where food is needed.

Although they have not worked out all the details, botanists believe that simple physical forces cause sap to move. Solutions tend to move from places of high concentration to those of low concentration. The highly concentrated sugars in leaves produce a pressure that pushes the sugary sap to stems, roots, and other areas where the concentration is lower. In some plants, this pressure is strong enough to cause sap to flow in the sieve tubes at the rate of 100 centimeters (40 inches) an hour.

Movement of gases and water depends on other factors, and on microscopic openings called stomata ("little mouths") that exist on plant stems and especially on leaves. Often they are most plentiful on the undersides of leaves. Their numbers vary greatly. A blade of grass may have 8,000 stomata in a square centimeter of its surface. A corn leaf has 15,500 and a cucumber leaf more than 60,000 stomata in the same area. Leaves on plants growing in shaded spots have fewer stomata than leaves in sunlit places.

Plants give off water vapor through their stomata, and gases flow in and out of these openings. Beyond the stomata, within the leaf, there are open spaces and channels among the cells through which air can reach the outer surface of the palisade cells. During daylight hours, the carbon dioxide needed for photosynthesis diffuses from this air into the palisade cells to the chloroplasts. Oxygen, a by-product of food making, sometimes flows out of stomata. Tree bark and the root surfaces of land plants also have openings, structurally different from stomata, that allow gases to enter and leave.

In 1980, a biologist in Michigan reported that he had discovered a sort of air-pumping system in yellow water-lily plants. His investigation showed that heat from the sun caused a rise in air pressure and water pressure within the open spaces inside young water-lily leaves. This pressure forced air to flow from the leaves to the rest of the plant, bringing vital oxygen to the lily's underwater food-storage stems (rhizomes). At night, the air pressure within the leaves returned to normal, and the air flow stopped. Whether heat from the sun helps pump gases through many other kinds of plants in this way is not known.

CELLS ON GUARD

The main job of the leaves—food making—influences the overall shape of a green plant; that is, the stems and leaves are usually arranged to expose as much leaf surface as possible to the sun. It also influences the structure of leaves. Except in arid climates, most leaves are thin and flat (to capture maximum solar energy), about 90 percent water, and dotted with holes to let air in. Since photosynthesis requires a steady flow of carbon dioxide gas, billions of open stomata are vital to a green plant's food supply. Carbon dioxide makes up only .03 percent of air, so large volumes of air must enter the leaves.

When a stoma is open to let air in, there is nothing to stop water from going out. This process is called transpiration. Tremendous amounts of water escape from stomata, especially on sunny, dry, windy days. A single corn plant may lose 200 kilograms (440 pounds) of water during a growing season of a few months. An acre of corn loses about 1,200 metric tons (1320 tons) of water in that time.

Normally, when a plant cell has more water entering than leaving, its big water sac, or vacuole, presses the cell's contents against its walls. This action is called turgor pressure, and such a cell is called turgid. Sometimes plants lose more water from their leaves than their roots take in. When the concentration of water molecules outside a cell lessens, the cell loses water through its membrane. The vacuole shrinks, and turgor pressure drops. Parts of the plant wilt, especially the leaves with their thin-walled cells. For it is water pressure within cells, as well as the skeleton of cell walls, that supports the plant and gives it form.

On a hot summer day, the leaves of many common garden plants wilt as they lose turgor pressure. At night, transpiration lessens, and water taken up by the roots replenishes the supply within cells so that they become turgid again. By morning the plants have usually assumed their normal shape.

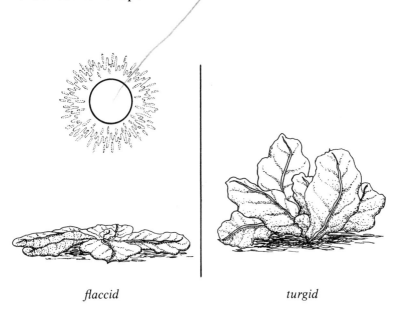

flaccid   *turgid*

Water helps to hold a plant up. Leaves wilt when the water pressure within their cells declines. As cell water pressure increases, the leaves regain their normal shape.

Loss of water from leaves is reduced somewhat by pairs of guard cells that enclose each stoma. When the guard cells are full of water, they bend outward, opening the stoma. When their turgor pressure lessens, they bend inward, and the stoma is nearly closed. Knowing this fact, it would seem that guard cells are controlled entirely by turgor in leaves and that they always shut stomata when the plant is losing water.

This is not the case. Stomata are usually closed at night and open in the day. They are often wide open near noon—

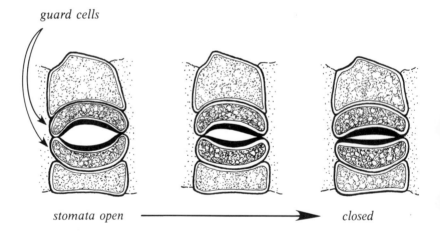

guard cells

stomata open ⟶ closed

The many thousands of stomata on each leaf are gateways through which gases, including water vapor, pass.

(18)

the time of greatest water loss. "Some guard cells!" you may say. But stomata must perform their other job: admitting carbon dioxide so food making can proceed. As botanist Arthur W. Galston wrote, "In effect, to get the benefits of photosynthesis, you have to accept the evils of transpiration."

Botanists have found that the concentration of carbon dioxide gas is one of the prime regulators of stomata size. When carbon dioxide levels within a leaf fall, a chemical change usually occurs that causes the guard cells to take in water, bend outward, and allow the stomata to open. Air flows in, replenishing the carbon dioxide.

Botanists do not fully understand the intricate stomatal system of plants. They know, however, that chemical messengers are involved and that guard cells act like tiny computers. Guard cells detect or receive information about water loss, carbon dioxide concentrations, and whether it is day or night. Based on these data, the guard cells of a leaf open or close stomata to provide the best balance between water loss and gas exchange.

Water lost by transpiration also benefits plants in at least one way. Leaves absorb great amounts of solar energy, and if evaporating water did not carry some of this heat energy off into the atmosphere, the cells would literally cook. In addition, nutrients become more concentrated within plants as water evaporates into the air.

MYSTERY OF THE RISING WATER

We know that plants take water into their roots, that it moves upward through vessels and tracheids, and that a large quantity is lost from leaves. What causes the water to rise? For centuries scientists puzzled over this question. According to the laws of physics, the pressure of the atmosphere is strong enough to raise a column of water about 9 meters (30 feet) when there is no friction. Some trees, however, stand over 90 meters (300 feet) tall. For water to reach the tops of these plants, a force at least ten times more powerful than atmospheric pressure must be involved.

In the 1800s some scientists thought that living plant cells acted like pumps. To test this idea, they used poison or boiling water to kill all the cells in 12-meter-long (40-foot-long) vines and in tree trunks. They found that water still moved upward—through dead cells. For a while, botanists also thought that a force from below, which they named root pressure, caused water to rise upward. Research eventually showed, however, that root pressure was lowest in the summer, when the greatest amount of water rose in plants.

Most botanists now agree that three physical forces bring water up through plants. The first force is produced by transpiration. As sunlight and wind cause water to evaporate from leaves, the water loss at the top of a plant creates a pull or negative pressure on the water below. The second force—cohesion—exists between water molecules; they are "sticky" and tend to cling together. The third force—adhesion—exists between water molecules and cell walls. Water tends to cling to the surface of cell walls. The combination of these three forces exerts a pull powerful enough to keep water moving up against the force of gravity—if necessary, all the way up to the top of a redwood.

CHAPTER THREE

Flowers and Pollinators

Two great groups of plants reproduce by seeds. Most successful by far are the angiosperms ("covered seeds"), which produce seeds from flowers. Flowering plants cover 90 percent of the earth's land surface and make up virtually all plants that humans and livestock eat. Yet they are relative newcomers in the history of life on this planet. They have existed for perhaps as little as 125 million years, whereas fossil remains of algae have been found in rocks that are 2 billion years old.

Flowers are fragile. Few of them remain whole long enough to become fossilized in rock, so we know little about their origins. We do know that flowering plants appeared sometime during the first half of the long reign of the dinosaurs. The dominant plants then were ferns and

A familiar cone protects mature seeds of such conifers as pines and
spruces, which are gymnosperms. At right are flowers of narcissus, an
angiosperm.

a second major group of seed-bearing plants, the gymnosperms ("naked seeds"), which included seed ferns, cycads
(plants that resemble palm trees), and conifers (trees that

bear their seeds within protective cones). Today the only common gymnosperms are conifers, including pines, spruces, firs, and hemlocks. The broad-leaved ginkgo, or maidenhair tree, is also a gymnosperm. It has been called a living fossil, since it is the sole surviving species of a gymnosperm group that flourished during the time of the dinosaurs.

The dinosaurs died out about 65 million years ago, but flowering plants have thrived and displaced most of the gymnosperms. Their dramatic and continued success is an enigma that many scientists have pondered. Charles Darwin called it an "abominable mystery."

Flowering plants have several characteristics that have no doubt contributed to their abundance and diversity. Their broad leaves catch more solar energy than the narrow leaves of most gymnosperms. Their vessel cells are slightly more efficient than the different water-carrying cells of most gymnosperms. But some gymnosperms do have vessel cells, and some have broad leaves. Thus the spectacular success of flowering plants is primarily due to another feature—their special reproductive organs, or flowers.

In most flowering plants, both male sex cells and female sex cells are present in each flower. The male sex cells begin to develop in structures called stamens and leave as pollen grains. Female sex cells (eggs, or ovules) develop within ovaries, which are enclosed in structures called pistils. The topmost part of the pistil, the stigma, is prominent and often sticky—a good target for pollen grains that fall, or are brought, near the pistil. When male sex cells from pollen grains reach the ovules in the ovary, fertilization occurs. The fertilized eggs then develop into seeds.

In some species, such as holly, either the flowers on one plant are all male (with stamens, but no pistils) or they are all female (pistils, but no stamens). Other plants, such as oak trees, have separate male and female flowers on the same plant. But the vast majority of flowering plants have male and female parts in each blossom.

Each flower's pollen simply has to reach its own ovules to produce seeds. This is called self-pollination. Over several generations, however, self-pollination may have harmful effects, producing smaller, less vigorous plants, for example. In the long run, plants benefit from cross-pollination, which brings together the characteristics of different plants of the same species. Since there are advantages to cross-pollination, many plants have developed ways in which they avoid pollinating themselves. For example, a plant's pollen may mature before its stigmas are receptive. The pollen can fertilize flowers of other plants, but not of its own. In other species the plant's stigmas may ripen before its pollen. Again, self-pollination is prevented. Also, flowers are often constructed in ways that make it difficult for self-pollination to occur.

Since plants are immobile, their long-term reproductive success depends on pollen somehow moving from one plant to another. Air currents and wind transport gymnosperm pollen. This mode of pollen transfer can be quite successful. In fact, the pollen of such flowering plants as grasses, sedges, sagebrushes, and several kinds of trees is carried on the wind. Studies using wind tunnels have shown that pinecones are shaped in ways that affect airflow patterns and help ensure that pine pollen reaches ovules of its own species.

Wind-pollinated plants produce great numbers of pollen grains—about 1 million for each egg cell available for fertilization. A single flower of a birch tree yields more than 5 million grains of pollen. The grains are lightweight and dry, so they do not stick together. Pollen can be carried 4,800 kilometers (3,000 miles) by the wind. But wind-borne pollen grains become widely dispersed within a few hundred feet of their source. A hit-or-miss process, wind pollination succeeds only because of the great num-

The earth's first flowers probably resembled magnolias, and may have been pollinated by beetles.

bers of male sex cells that are produced.

Insects are more reliable pollen carriers. Some species existed when flowering plants evolved; beetles, for example, were common. Botanists believe that the earliest flowers probably looked somewhat like magnolias or buttercups, with wide-open petals and numerous stamens

(27)

covered with abundant pollen. Insects that visit such flowers eat as much as 90 percent of the pollen, but accidentally carry some grains away with them to other flowers. Biologists believe that this form of pollination was a crucial factor in the early success of flowering plants. Today, landscapes are covered with plants that must be pollinated by insects in order to survive.

As flowering plants began to thrive as a result of insect pollination, they gradually changed in ways that took advantage of their insect visitors. They produced fewer pollen grains, and these grains were sticky, so they clung easily to the insects' bodies.

Some insects eat egg cells as readily as they do pollen, and the ovules of the earliest flowering plants probably had little protection. Those individual plants that had some ovule covering were more likely to reproduce successfully than those without. Eventually, all flowering plants developed protective enclosures for their egg cells— the ovaries within the pistil. Today the fertilized eggs of all these plants form seeds that are enclosed in a protective coating. So all flowering plants are classified as angiosperms ("enclosed seeds").

The plant tissues that protect ovules also form barriers to the male sex cells within pollen grains. This obstacle is overcome by remarkable structures called pollen tubes. When a pollen grain reaches the stigma of a flower, a chemical receptor in the stigma's cuticle is able to tell— from proteins on the pollen grain's surface—whether the pollen is from the same species of plant. If the pollen is "alien," it does not develop. If the pollen is from the plant's own species, it receives a chemical message or

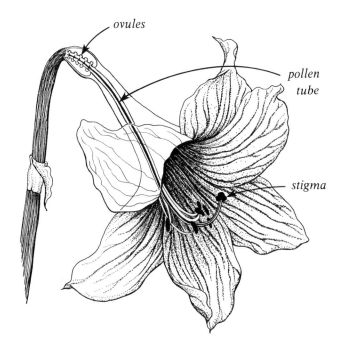

For fertilization to occur, a pollen tube must grow from the stigma to the well-protected ovules.

stimulus from the stigma. Within a few minutes the pollen grain takes up water from the stigma, swells, and produces a threadlike pollen tube that breaks through the cuticle of the stigma and burrows through tissue until it reaches the flower's ovary. Some pollen tubes are remarkably long. A petunia pollen grain produces a tube that is about 900 times the size of the grain itself.

Insects often leave several pollen grains of the same species on a flower stigma. When this occurs, a race to reach the ovary takes place among the developing pollen tubes. The pollen grain with the most vigorous, fastest-growing tube fertilizes the egg, and its characteristics are passed on to the next generation of plants. Some botanists believe that the competition among pollen tubes contributes to the great diversity and success of flowering plants.

THIS WAY TO THE NECTAR

Many of the insects that evolved millions of years ago—including flies, bees, wasps, beetles, moths, and butterflies—are attracted to pollen or nectar as food. Flowering plants evolved in ways that took advantage of insect pollinators and other animals as well. The shape, color, and scent of flower parts insure that certain insects will visit a blossom for food, picking up or leaving pollen in the process. An expert in flower pollination can walk through a field or garden and say, "There's a bee-pollinated flower; that's a moth-pollinated flower."

Many bee flowers have parts that serve as landing platforms. Since bees have long tongues (sucking tubes), the petals of flowers they pollinate often form a long cylinder. Rows of "hairs" or other structures inside the cylinder may keep smaller insects from the nectar, which is produced at the bottom. Bees have sensitive odor receptors in their antennae, so most bee flowers are scented. Also, most bee flowers are either blue, yellow, or purple—colors that bees see. Red is thought to appear black to bees. They visit some red flowers—poppies, for instance—because the flowers also reflect ultraviolet light, which is visible to bees.

Some flowers have colored markings that seem to advertise, or lead pollinators to, their food source. Patterns of lines, dots, or solid colors lure insects to the spot where they will inadvertently pollinate the flower. These markings are called nectar guides or honey guides. We can see them on violets, irises, jewelweed, and other flowers. Some honey guides, however, reflect ultraviolet light, which is visible to many pollinators but not to humans. The petals

Tests show that pollinating insects can see ultraviolet light, which is invisible to humans. A bee may see dark ultraviolet markings around the center of a buttercup flower.

of the marsh marigold and black-eyed Susan, for example, appear to be solid yellow to people. To bees, however, the petals are two-tone, with ultraviolet near the blossom's center, at the source of food.

Some plants are adapted for pollination by moths. Their petals form long tubes, matching the long tongues of moths. These flowers tend to be white or light colored, showing up well at night when moths are active. Some open only at night, and some emit a strong scent then.

Moth flowers have no landing platforms, since moths usually hover in the air as they feed.

Many kinds of flies are pollinators. They tend to be attracted to rotting meat or other decaying matter; so, as might be expected, fly-pollinated flowers tend to be dark brown, purple, or green in color, and they may smell awful. One fly plant, the wild arum, is shaped in such a way that small flies must crawl inside, where they are temporarily trapped. Once the arum's pollen-bearing stamens mature, the flies can escape by crawling over them. In the process they become dusted with pollen.

Nutritious pollen and nectar attract animal pollinators other than insects. The flowers of some tropical plants have adapted in ways that lure birds or bats. Birds see color, but have a poor sense of smell; thus bird flowers are often bright red or orange and have little scent. Bat flowers open in the evening and close during the day. They have wide openings, foul odors, and strong parts that can withstand clutching claws as the bats eat pollen or sip nectar.

In nature there are many paths to success, and some creatures seek shortcuts. Some bees, other insects, and birds pierce or cut through the bases of flower petals and take nectar without touching pollen-bearing stamens. One tropical nectar-robbing bird has an apt name: the masked flower-piercer. Hummingbirds successfully pollinate most of the blossoms that the flower-piercer leaves alone.

Many remarkable matches have formed between flowers and their pollinators. Some have evolved together, or coevolved, until the plant species has just one species of pollinator. Charles Darwin discovered one of these "lock-and-key" relationships in Madagascar. An orchid he found there had about 4 centimeters (1.6 inches) of nectar at the bottom of a flower tube 30 centimeters (12 inches) long. Darwin said that there must be a species of moth in Madagascar with a sucking tongue that could uncoil to about 30 centimeters. Entomologists scoffed at the idea. Many years later, such a moth was found.

SNUG AS A BUG IN A BLOSSOM

As interest in the science of ecology has increased, many people have become aware of how living things depend on one another as flowering plants and their pollinators do. The subject of coevolution between plants and animals intrigues biologists and is under scientific investigation in the wild. One possible instance of the mutual dependence between flowers and insects, however, was discovered by accident.

(34)

Roger Knutson, a biologist in Iowa, wondered why many spring wild flowers had certain characteristics— their blossoms were bowl or saucer shaped, their petals light colored, and their many stamens fuzzy. The flowers often moved so their centers faced the sun in its path across the sky. Their shapes and colors seemed to be adapted to reflect sunlight to their centers. One cold April morning, Knutson measured the temperature in the flower centers of prairie pasqueflowers. He was surprised to find it to be 7½ to 10 degrees Celsius (14 to 18 degrees Fahrenheit) warmer than the surrounding air. The flowers cooled soon after they were shaded.

Apparently, the design of these flowers is such that they capture and retain heat from the sun. In every blossom, Knutson found bees, beetles, and other flying insects. Insects often spent nights within the blossoms, which closed at night. Knutson also learned that pasqueflowers (and many other spring wild flowers) produce little pollen. Insects may be attracted to them more for warmth than food, he suggests. By successfully capturing warmth from the sun, the flowers attract pollinators without needing to use their own food energy to produce much pollen.

This possibility raises questions about another kind of spring wild flower—the skunk cabbage. It, too, provides

(35)

insects a warm place in a cold time. Its heat is not absorbed directly from sunlight, but comes from a short, thick, flower-bearing structure called the spadix, which is partly enclosed by a dark-colored, leaflike sheath known as a spathe. As a skunk cabbage spadix "burns" food, it produces heat energy.

When Knutson measured temperatures of skunk cabbage spadices, he found them to be 20 to 35 degrees Celsius

In the early spring, insects are attracted to skunk cabbage flowers, which are often much warmer than the air temperature.

(36 to 63 degrees Fahrenheit) warmer than air temperature. Furthermore, skunk cabbage spadices maintained a
constant temperature, generating more heat when the air
temperature fell and less when it rose.

The warmth of a skunk cabbage flower may be simply
the by-product of the burning of food energy as the spadix
develops and grows. The heat nevertheless attracts honey-
bees and other pollinators during early spring, when the
insects may find a warm place as appealing as food. Thus,
it seems that the heat-producing spadix may be another
unusual way by which insects are induced to transport
pollen from one flower to another.

CHAPTER FOUR

Seeds and Clones

Insects and other flying animals enable flowering plants to crossbreed and produce seeds. But when seeds fall beneath the parent plant, conditions may keep them from sprouting; or if they sprout, the seedlings may compete intensely for water and other needs. Immobile plants and their offspring all benefit from seed dispersal and have evolved in ways that help this to happen.

Some dinosaurs undoubtedly fed on the seeds of early angiosperms, but it is difficult to say whether they helped spread seeds. There is no doubt, however, that the evolution of birds was a key factor in seed dispersal. Birds, which may have evolved from small dinosaurs, were the first living things that could carry seeds rapidly over great distances. They were able to spread flowering plants across rivers, seas, mountains, and other barriers to new habitats. The success of angiosperms and birds seems to be linked, and today birds still play a key role in seed dispersal. To a lesser extent, so do mammals.

When people think of an animal carrying seeds, they usually picture a nut in a squirrel's mouth, a seed stuck to fur or feathers, or seeds hidden in a bit of mud between an animal's toes. Many seeds are transported in such ways, on the outside of an animal. Many others travel inside animals.

Seeds a bird or mammal swallows whole are often not digested. Food passes rather quickly through the digestive tract of warm-blooded animals, and viable seeds (seeds capable of developing) emerge in their wastes. Summer-time droppings of foxes, bears, and raccoons, for example, commonly contain seeds of berries and other fruit. So do the droppings of berry-eating birds. Passage through an animal's digestive tract often helps prepare seeds for germination. Hard seed coats are softened. If such seeds fall in suitable places, they readily sprout and grow.

All the objects we commonly call fruits—apples, peaches, berries, cherries, bananas, oranges—represent ways to attract animals that will scatter seeds. Such fruits contain hard-coated seeds that are surrounded by nutri-

Milkweed seeds disperse through the air, while those of many fruits travel through birds and emerge in their wastes.

tious and colorful pulp or flesh, which usually gives off an appealing odor. Many of them are colored in shades of red, which is especially attractive to birds. Unripe fruit has a different smell, its taste is often bitter, and its color often green. Only when the hidden seeds are mature and ready for dispersal does the surrounding flesh become ripe and alluring. (The cause of this change is described in Chapter 5.) Ripe fruits are beautiful, but, as Charles Darwin wrote, "This beauty serves merely as a guide to birds and beasts, in order that the fruit may be devoured and the manured seeds disseminated."

The colors, tastes, and odors of fruits are all the result of millions of years of coevolution with certain fruit-eating animals. In most cases the same animals feed on the same kinds of fruit today. In some, however, the fruit-eating animal has become extinct. This may be true of the original avocado eaters. Once avocado trees grew wild in parts of Central America, but now only cultivated forms exist. Avocado fruits have oily, highly nutritious flesh surrounding a pit (seed) that is too big for most of the existing wildlife in Central America to swallow whole and pass undigested.

It seems likely that avocado fruits coevolved with creatures big enough to gulp down whole avocados without harming the large pit. No such animals live in Central America now, but mastodons, glyptodonts, and giant ground sloths were plentiful there until about 10,000 years ago, when they became extinct. Avocados might have died out too had not Indians reached Central America a few thousand years ago and begun raising them for food.

Another plant may not be so fortunate. It is a tree called tambalacoque, or *Calvaria major*, which grows on Mauritius, an island in the western Indian Ocean. Although the *Calvaria* was once common, now only a few trees, more than 300 years old, are left. No young trees exist, even though the old survivors produce seeds each year. The seeds measure 50 millimeters (2 inches) in diameter, and each is enclosed in an extremely thick seed coat. Even when planted under the most favorable conditions in a tree nursery, the seeds do not sprout unless parts of their hard coats have been worn away.

The mystery of the disappearing *Calvaria* was investigated by Stanley Temple, a wildlife ecologist at the University of Wisconsin. Historical records show that a few centuries ago, Mauritius had a creature that had probably coevolved with the *Calvaria* tree. It was the dodo—a huge, flightless, seed-eating bird that became extinct in 1681.

The dodo had a gizzard that contained large stones, enabling it to crush food. According to Stanley Temple,

Dodoes may have played a key role in the reproduction of *Calvaria* trees. Their gizzards could weaken the tough seed coats, thus enabling the seeds to sprout.

a dodo crushed seeds with thin coats and digested them. The *Calvaria* evolved such a thick coat, however, that some of its seeds could withstand a grinding in a dodo's gizzard. Many birds with gizzards hold hard objects, including tough-coated seeds, in their gizzards for several days. Eventually the seeds pass through the digestive tract

(43)

and are excreted, or they are regurgitated. Fossil *Calvaria* seeds have been found among the fossil skeletons of dodoes.

Temple believes that *Calvaria* seed coats became so tough that the seeds germinated *only* after their coats had been scarred and weakened in the gizzard of a dodo. To test this idea, he force-fed some *Calvaria* seeds to turkeys, which have gizzards. The turkeys crushed seven of seventeen seed coats in their gizzards and digested the seeds. The other ten seeds the turkeys regurgitated or passed in their droppings. The action of the gizzards had worn and weakened the seed coats. Temple planted these ten seeds, and three sprouted. They may have been the first *Calvaria* seeds to germinate in more than 300 years, since the last dodo died.

WAITING TO GERMINATE

Besides traveling in the insides and on the outsides of animals, seeds disperse through the air and on the water. They have evolved wind-catching designs: wings, parachutes, propellers, gliders, disks. Seeds are fired from springlike devices or from ovaries that explode. Coconuts and sea beans, with air cavities that make them buoyant,

may float in the ocean for months, over hundreds of miles, before reaching suitable shores on which to sprout.

Most seeds, however, spend much less time as travelers. Dispersal usually takes up only a tiny fraction of their lives. The rest is spent in the soil, waiting for conditions that are favorable for germination. The ability of seeds to survive, often for many years, is an extraordinary adaptation.

Each seed from an angiosperm contains an embryo plant. Surrounding the embryo is tissue called endosperm, a food supply for the embryo. Endosperm is the starchy pulp we see—and eat—inside a kernel of corn or grain of wheat.

Both the endosperm and embryo are enclosed in a seed coat that develops from a flower's ovule. These seed parts grow to a certain stage on the mother plant and then stop. Botanists have recently discovered that a growth-inhibiting hormone called abscisic acid causes this change to occur (see Chapter 5). As the seed parts grow, the concentration of abscisic acid increases within a seed, the embryo stops growing, the water content of the seed drops, and the seed coat hardens. Now the seed is ready for the main activity of its life—waiting.

There are good reasons to wait. Many seeds mature in

the late summer and early autumn. If they germinated right away, the seedlings might die with the first frost. Successful germination of many desert seeds depends on waiting for the rainy season. The surface of desert soils is peppered with seeds of annual wild flowers that lie dormant until watered. The amount of water is critical; it must be sufficient to enable the seedlings to grow into mature plants and produce another generation of seeds. A

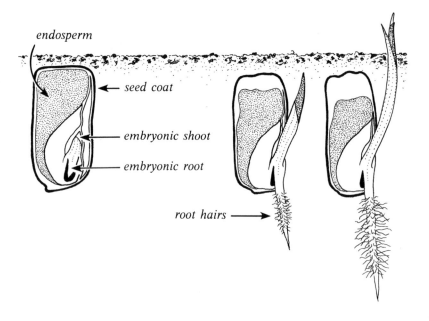

endosperm

← seed coat

— embryonic shoot

— embryonic root

root hairs ⟶

The first growth of a young corn plant is sustained by the seed's stored food, the endosperm.

(46)

light rain shower that wets seeds a little will not stimulate germination, but a heavy downpour will. The water washes away growth inhibitors from seed coats, and embryo plants can then begin to develop.

Other kinds of seeds need a few weeks of near-freezing temperatures to set the stage for germination. Chilling causes the amount of growth inhibitor to decline, so the seed is ready to sprout once such needs as warmth and moisture are met.

Water was once thought to be the key ingredient for seed germination. Many seeds can, in fact, be induced to sprout by continuously running water over their coats. But seeds can have plenty of water around them in the soil and still remain dormant. Botanists have been surprised to find that seeds buried in the soil often contain plentiful water. The water enables the embryo to remain sufficiently active so that any cell damage during dormancy can be repaired. Such seeds survive longer than those stored in laboratory jars. It seems that seeds in dry storage lose their viability because they cannot carry on basic repairs and maintenance.

Open fields may contain as many as 100,000 dormant seeds per square meter. They lie buried only a short depth in moist soil; yet they do not sprout. Why? The reasons are not completely understood, but light seems to be a critical factor for some species of plants. In the 1960s botanists discovered that a mature seed taken from its parent plant, watered, and then placed in the dark would sprout. But when seeds of the same kind were buried in moist soil, they did not sprout. Burial caused a change

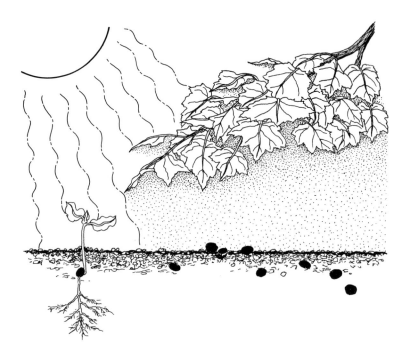

Seeds can detect the colors of light reaching them, and some kinds will not sprout if most of the available red light from the sun is blocked by leaves overhead.

(48)

within the seeds that could be reversed only by exposure to light. This is a great benefit to buried seeds—they are stimulated to sprout only after a farmer's plow or other disturbance brings them to the surface. If seeds sprouted while deeply buried they might not have enough stored food energy for growth to the surface.

Further research showed that these light-sensitive seeds detect the colors of light reaching them. If the red portion of sunlight is filtered out, the seeds will not germinate. The leaves of plants absorb red light as photosynthesis occurs. Thus, a thick canopy of green leaves allows very little red light to reach the ground. Some kinds of plant seedlings flourish in such low-light conditions; most, however, have poor chances of survival. It is better for these seeds to remain dormant until the conditions are better. When green leaves are not blocking sunlight from the soil surface, the seeds detect plentiful red light, which causes a pigment called phytochrome to change to a form that stimulates seeds to germinate.

Some seeds, especially of short-lived weeds, can lie buried for many years, waiting for favorable light. Botanists at archeological digs sometimes find seeds that were buried in old soil layers of known ages. Sites people occupied 600 years ago yield seeds that sprout and grow into normal plants. Near Jutland, Denmark, seeds were found in soil more than 1,700 years old. Several of them germinated. One was a plant called lamb's-quarters, a common weed of gardens and farmland. (Lamb's-quarters, a highly nutritious relative of spinach, is considered by some a fine food.)

Old or new, once a seed absorbs enough water—50 to 60 percent of its weight—the embryo begins to grow. The endosperm provides food for cell growth. The first root pushes downward, the first shoot reaches upward, the first seed leaf or leaves unfold, and food making begins. A new plant is born.

CLONING AROUND

Not all angiosperms rely on flowers, pollen, seed production, and seed germination in order to reproduce. Anyone who cultivates a garden knows another way in which many plants propagate—vegetative reproduction, or, as some botanists now refer to it, clonal growth or cloning. In this process, a new plant grows from a part of a parent plant by means of a bulb, tuber, cutting, or runner. The offspring is usually a genetically identical daughter.

Strawberries often reproduce by cloning. Toward the

Each strawberry runner may become a new, independent plant.

end of summer a strawberry plant sends out long stems called runners over the soil surface. Eventually the tip of a runner turns upward and produces a cluster of leaves. Roots grow downward from this point on the stem. Once the new plant is well established, the runner that connected it to its parent dies. The new strawberry plant is then totally independent. Mint and lily of the valley reproduce in a similar way, though their offspring sprout from underground food-storage stems called rhizomes.

A grass plant can reproduce by sending out lateral buds called tillers. Tips of tillers take root and form new clumps of grass. Eventually the tiller connection between mother and daughter becomes dormant and then decays. Swedish botanist Daniel J. Harberd studied this form of cloning in grasslands. In one pasture he was able to identify the grass plants produced by the tillering of a single plant (which probably grew from a seed). Clonal growth of the grass plants had stretched more than 216 meters (240 yards) from their source. According to Harberd's estimate of the rate of tillering, the clonal growth had begun about a thousand years before his study.

Older clones have been identified in Minnesota and Utah. New aspen trees can develop from buds that sprout from the out-reaching roots of a mature tree. If a forest fire destroys the parent tree, many such clones sprout from its root system. Clonal growth from one Utah aspen tree produced more than 47,000 other trees. Botanists believe that an aspen grove covering several acres in Minnesota is totally the result of cloning that began after the retreat of the last glacier, 8,000 years ago.

If we think of all those aspen trees as parts of one plant, then we will have to revise our ideas about how long a plant can live. Whether we call it growth or reproduction, cloning is common among flowering plants, even though they can reproduce by seeds. For certain plants under certain conditions, cloning has advantages over sexual reproduction. Perhaps the most important is the connection between the parent plant and its offspring. As a new grass plant develops, the flow of food from its parent through the tiller lessens and then stops. But the tiller stays alive for a while. If the new grass plant is injured severely by mowing or grazing, food flows from the parent again and continues until the new plant has recovered and is producing its own food from new leaves.

CHAPTER FIVE

Sensing and Responding

Plant stems grow up and roots grow down. But how does a plant tell up from down? And then, what causes it to grow in the right direction? Botanists have long wondered about these questions.

It is obviously beneficial for a green plant to send its roots down into the earth—to anchor itself and to absorb water and minerals from the soil. Also, it is vital that its leaves be aboveground in the sunlight. Thus, immobile plants, as well as mobile animals, must have a way to orient themselves in the world. Gravity is the force that influences the orientation of both. The response of plants to gravity is called geotropism ("earth bending"). Roots grow toward the pull of gravity (positive geotropism) and stems away from it (negative geotropism). Plants have demonstrated this process many times in laboratories. Further, when seeds were allowed to germinate in satellites high above the earth, where the force of gravity is low, the roots of the seedlings did not grow toward the center of the earth as they normally do.

Humans and other animals are able to distinguish up from down, and keep their balance as well, because of the movements of little objects called statoliths that are attached to sensitive hair cells within their inner ears. Plants have statoliths too. They are heavy starch grains found in special cells located at the growing tips of roots and probably elsewhere in plants. Normally the force of gravity keeps these heavy objects lying at the bottoms of their cells. If a plant is tipped on its side, the statoliths respond to the pull of gravity and roll up against another cell wall.

As the statoliths press against the cell membrane, they stimulate changes in the concentrations of growth hormones. A hormone is a substance that is produced in small amounts in one part of a plant, then transported to another part where it has some special effect. It is a sort of chemical messenger. When a root or stem is tipped from its normal vertical position, the concentration of growth hormones within the cells changes and causes the stem or root to right itself. For example, soon after a stem is laid down horizontally, the concentration of growth-stimulating hormones on its lower side increases measurably. This causes the cells there to elongate, and the stem curves upward.

Instead of having two centers of balance, as humans

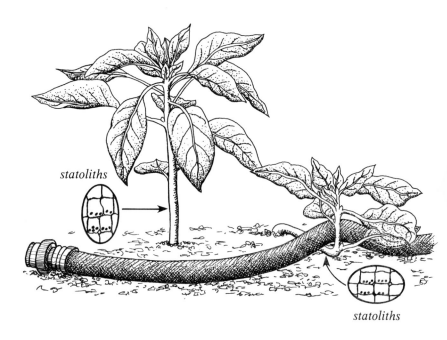

statoliths

statoliths

When a young pepper plant is accidentally tipped over by a garden hose, its statoliths fall from their normal position and stimulate growth so that the plant stem rights itself again.

do—one inside each inner ear—plants seem to have statolith gravity detectors wherever growth occurs. These detectors affect plants of all species, from a geranium
houseplant that is accidentally tipped over to a great tree
that is partly felled by a windstorm. Just as the geranium
stem rights itself, eventually the top of the tree's main
trunk curves upward, away from the pull of gravity.

Responding to gravity is only one kind of plant movement. Many plant species move in daily rhythms. Some
hold their leaves open and horizontal in the day, then
vertical and closed at night. Some plants respond to touch.
Insect-eating plants react quickly enough to trap their
prey. For many years we have also known that green
plants grow toward sunlight. This is called positive phototropism (bending toward light). Most houseplants turn
their leaves toward windows. The leaves of a common
low-growing weed called mallow slowly move so they face
the sun all day. At dusk the leaves turn in the opposite
direction, ready to catch the morning sun.

Plants contain pigments that are sensitive to amounts
and qualities of light, and many studies have been conducted on how plants respond to light. Yet, as recently as
1974, biologists discovered another way in which plants
orient themselves by distinguishing light from dark. They

also answered a question that had baffled many people: How do vines find objects to climb? Charles Darwin believed that vine seedlings accomplished this by growing away from light. Others claimed that seedlings located supports to climb by random searching.

Donald Strong, Jr., an insect ecologist, recalled this old question while doing research in Costa Rica. He and his student-assistant, Thomas Ray, Jr., who were studying insects on a banana plantation, were intrigued by a sight along their path—hundreds of little vines converging from all directions on a tree trunk.

Strong and Ray thought about the life of a vine seedling in a tropical rain forest. To grow into a mature plant, the seedling must grow from its dark rooting site to sunlight high overhead. Only by reaching a tree trunk can the seedling accomplish this. As Ray later wrote,

> To understand the problem of finding a tree, imagine yourself to be a seedling on the shady forest floor. Looking around, you see the light-green canopy above, and silhouetted against this are the long, dark tree trunks. The key word is dark. An efficient way of getting to the nearest tree is to grow toward darkness, a response . . . that is very unusual for organisms that depend directly on solar energy.

(58)

The biologists called this phenomenon skototropism (growth toward darkness), which is not the same as growth away from light. In their experiments, vine seedlings grew toward a dark object on the plants' horizon, not necessarily directly opposite a source of light. The larger the tree trunk, the greater the distance from which vine seedlings grew toward it. Once a seedling reached the base of a tree, it ceased to orient itself by skototropism and began to climb toward the sun.

Farmers have long known that if a pole is placed near a bean plant, the bean will find the pole and grow up it. They call this occurrence "beans chasing poles." Whether skototropism leads all kinds of climbing plants to their supports remains to be seen.

After witnessing a vine seedling change directions in pursuit of a pole that was moved several times, one man wrote, "It shows the consciousness of plants. It proves that they think."

We now know that this is untrue. Bean plants need only light-sensitive pigments and the ability to grow in order to reach a pole to climb. Plants do not think, but a century ago so little was known about the causes of plant movements that it was tempting to suspect that they did. Charles Darwin wrote that the growing tip of a root "acts like the brain of one of the lower animals." Though he made this comparison, he did not seriously consider that plants had brains. He did, however, conduct some simple

Hundreds of tropical vine seedlings converge on a dark tree trunk, which they detect with light-sensitive pigments.

(60)

but carefully designed experiments of geotropism in roots, discovering "it is the tip alone which is acted on, and that this part transmits some influence to the adjoining parts, causing them to curve downward."

The influence Darwin detected was later found to be a hormone called auxin. Its discovery in 1928, and later findings of its vital growth-stimulating effects, led botanists and biochemists to look for other hormonal influences in plants. We now know that hormones control almost every phase of plant life. They do not enable plants to think, but their effects are no less remarkable.

CHEMICAL MESSENGERS

Auxin plays a key role in plant growth. Produced by cells in growing stem tips and young leaves, the hormone moves to areas where cells are capable of growing longer and stimulates this growth. It causes parts of the plant to bend in response to gravity, light, touch, and other outside effects. Auxin also stimulates cell division. After pollination of a flower, great amounts of auxin are present in the ovary as it develops into a fruit. In fact, auxin can be used to stimulate development of a seedless tomato from a tomato flower that has not been pollinated.

Long before the discovery of auxin, rice farmers in Japan noticed the effects of another growth hormone. Occasionally certain rice plants grew to extraordinary length, though they seldom flowered. The farmers believed such plants suffered from the "foolish seedling" disease. Eventually a Japanese botanist discovered that a fungus called *Gibberella* produced a substance that stimulated this "foolish" growth. The substance was called gibberellin. Japanese scientists made progress in identifying the substance chemically, but their research ceased during and for several years after World War II.

Since 1950, however, much has been learned about the gibberellins—a group of more than fifty closely related chemical compounds that occur naturally in plants. Since they are quite similar, one kind of gibberellin can be changed easily to another by a plant. One, called gibberellic acid, causes the great elongation of stems the Japanese farmers observed on rice plants. It also stimulates rapid elongation of flower stalks and the flowering of many plants.

Botanists have found that gibberellins increase within apple seeds as they mature. They suspect that these hormones help control seed development. Gibberellins also seem to be involved in seed germination. When dormant seeds are soaked in gibberellins, they soon sprout.

Recently, Danish scientists found that gibberellins also play a role in the downward growth of roots, which auxin is already known to influence. In an experiment they split some horizontally growing roots and vertically growing roots in half lengthwise and then measured the concentration of gibberellins in the different sections. The gibberellins were evenly distributed in the roots that had been growing vertically. In the roots that had been growing horizontally, gibberellins were most abundant in the upper halves. By stimulating the cells there to elongate, the hormones would cause roots to bend downward.

Research has also shown that some cells are sensitive to gibberellins whereas others respond to auxin. No one knows why. The chemical interactions of plant hormones are extremely complex. Some seem to work against one another. Some combine effects with other hormones and produce great growth. Hormones called cytokinins, for example, interact with auxin, sometimes stimulating growth, sometimes discouraging it. Cytokinins are produced in roots and then flow to other plant parts.

Auxin and a hormone called ethylene sometimes work together. Ethylene is a gas plants produce naturally. It plays a major role in the ripening of fruit and in the death of flower petals and leaves. When flower petals wilt and droop, ethylene is the cause. In such short-lived blossoms as day lilies and morning glories, exposure to a few hours of sunlight stimulates the production of ethylene. In some other flowers, including orchids, the act of pollination causes ethylene to be produced. The hormone soon causes cells to lose turgor so that whole petals collapse.

Ethylene is the main hormone controlling leaf fall, or abscission, from plants. It affects a special zone of cells at the base of a leaf's stalk, or petiole, where it attaches to a stem. An old leaf can snap off at any time, but all or nearly all the leaves of deciduous trees and shrubs fall off in autumn. Decreasing day length triggers changes in the abscission zone of each leaf. Concentrations of cytokinins and auxin decline. Ethylene then hastens the aging of cells in the abscission zone, causing their walls to weaken. It also causes the petiole cells nearest the stem to swell with water, which puts pressure on the neighboring weakened cells. A combination of this force and the weight of the leaf itself eventually causes the petiole to break off.

Ethylene's most vital role is in ripening fruit. The attraction of ripened fruit, after all, induces animals to disperse seeds. Usually the flesh of a fruit develops from a flower ovary, influenced by auxin and gibberellins. Once

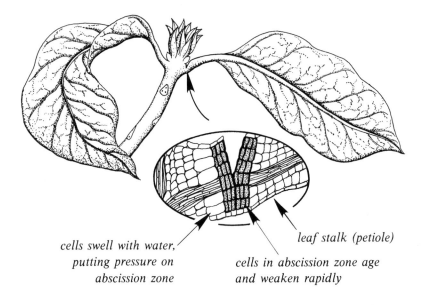

cells swell with water,
putting pressure on
abscission zone

leaf stalk (petiole)

cells in abscission zone age
and weaken rapidly

Ethylene produces these changes in the cells of leaf stalks, causing leaves to drop from plants.

at full size, however, a fruit is still hard and inedible. Ethylene changes that. Under its influence, cell walls weaken, and flavors and scents are formed. Exactly how ethylene causes these changes is unknown. In bananas the hormone seems to serve only as a trigger for the ripening process. In such fruits as apples and pears, it apparently must be present during the whole process.

Not all plant hormones stimulate growth. Some stop activity, or induce plants and seeds to lie dormant.

(65)

Growth inhibitors are vital to the survival of plants and seeds under adverse conditions. They are present in the fruit that surrounds seeds, on seed coats, or within seeds. Abscisic acid is the best-known guard against premature germination of seeds. It is also the chemical messenger that causes stomata to close when leaves are losing too much water. At such times, its concentration in guard cells may increase ten times in a few minutes.

Even though botanists do not fully understand how plant hormones work, synthetic versions of these chemicals are now commonly used by plant breeders, orchardists, farmers, and food-marketing companies. Synthetic plant hormones affect many of the foods we eat. Sprays of auxin, for example, are used to prevent fruits from dropping from trees before harvest. Gibberellic acid is sprayed on seedless grapes as they develop to stimulate the growth of large grapes and large bunches. Gibberellins are also used to increase the length of celery, rhubarb, and sugarcane stalks.

Synthetic hormones that inhibit growth also have many uses. They prevent stored potatoes and onions from sprouting and retard the stem growth of lilies, poinsettias, and other ornamental plants. Normally such flowers have tall stems, but commercial growers find that most customers prefer more compact plants. In addition, growth inhibitors are used to produce short-stemmed wheat plants that do not fall over from the weight of their ripe seed heads. This practice helps reduce loss of wheat when fields are harvested.

Commercial growers apply their knowledge about ethylene in two contrasting ways: they use the gas to ripen fruit, or stifle the gas so that ripening is delayed. Bananas, which are harvested while still green, hard, and starchy, are exposed to ethylene to trigger their ripening. The second practice is often used on apples. The McIntosh apples we buy in June were picked the previous September. They were kept in cool, enclosed storage places that have less oxygen and more nitrogen and carbon dioxide than usual. The latter two gases suppress the ripening effects of ethylene. The apples ripen when taken from storage, though they lack the distinctive flavor and aroma of fresh fruit. There is no evidence that application of ethylene or other synthetic hormones to food plants is harmful to human health.

People sometimes use ethylene to ripen fruit at home. If a ripe fruit is placed with unripe fruit in an enclosed space, ethylene from the ripe fruit will stimulate the ripening of the others. A pineapple houseplant can be induced to blossom if put in a plastic bag with a ripe banana. No doubt further uses, minor and major, will be found for hormones as more is learned about these chemicals that guide the lives of plants.

RESPONDING TO THE WORLD AROUND THEM

Hormones are involved in many different plant movements, though how they work is often not well understood. To understand the role of hormones in rapid growth movements, botanists have studied how the thin tendrils of garden peas grasp holds. The tip of a tendril first forms a coil around a supporting object. Then the rest of the tendril forms a coil in space, which causes the plant to be pulled closer to the object. Tendrils uncurl if they lose touch with their support. If undisturbed, however, part of the tendril eventually strengthens with the woody substance lignin.

Touch stimulates tendril curling, though steady contact, rather than a brief touch, is necessary. A tendril can be made to curl by stroking it a few times. Botanists have found that curling results from the uneven growth of various cells that auxin and ethylene seem to control, though

Within minutes of touching an object, a tendril begins to grow longer
and form coils around it.

how the hormones interact is not yet known. Perhaps the
greatest mystery about tendril curling is how it happens
so quickly. A touch on a pea tendril's tip can cause cells

(69)

to elongate elsewhere in the tendril within two minutes. Auxin does not travel that fast through plant tissues, so a faster messenger must be involved.

The identity of this messenger is suspected from the studies of even faster plant movements among insect-eating plants. Some, such as the pitcher plant, passively trap insects that enter with obstacles that make escape difficult. Others are active. Venus's-flytrap snaps shut on its prey. Each flytrap leaf has two halves, hinged together, that normally lie in the open position. Each half has stiff bristles along its edge and three sensitive trigger "hairs" on its upper surface. An insect that touches one of these hairs triggers a chemical reaction, which sends an electrical signal to the leaf cells.

One signal produces no action. It could be a false alarm— an insect that quickly left or an object that fell by accident onto the flytrap. But two or more signals from trigger hairs stimulate action. Some leaf cells expand rapidly and cause the two leaf halves to snap shut in less than a tenth of a second. As the insect struggles and touches the triggers, more electrical signals are sent to the leaf cells. The trap closes more tightly. Digestive chemicals are secreted from leaf cells. A flytrap leaf needs about a week to digest most of a large insect; then its two halves open wide again.

Electrical signals also cause quick movements in *Mimosa pudica*, the sensitive plant. The mimosa does not respond as quickly as Venus's-flytrap, but the effect is spectacular. A touch to a mimosa leaflet somehow triggers electrical signals that travel to thin-walled cells where the water balance is upset, turgor is lost, and leaflets droop. A few touches can cause every single leaflet and twig to fold up.

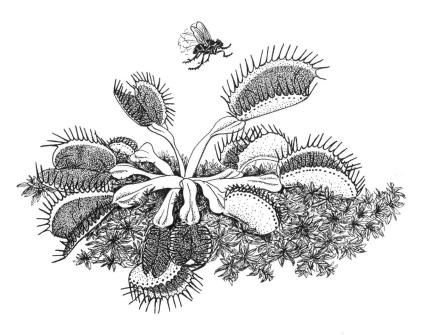

When an insect touches trigger hairs and stimulates electrical signals, the leaf of a Venus's-flytrap quickly snaps shut.

The quick movements of the mimosa plant and Venus's-flytrap are unusual. In comparison, the coiling of a pea tendril seems slow, and so do leaf movements of other plants. The redwood sorrel, for example, grows in the deep shade of the forest floor and folds its leaves when struck by direct sunlight. Although exposure to bright sunlight causes movement to begin in ten seconds, the sorrel leaves need six minutes in which to fold completely. Most plants take much longer than this to change the positions of their leaves or stems.

The plants all around us—trees, garden vegetables, houseplants—survive very well without being able to move quickly; thus they have not developed the ability to transmit speedy signals. Even the swiftest electrical signals in plants are terribly slow and of much lower voltage than those in animals, which have nerve cells especially adapted to produce and conduct electrical signals. All plants, however, send and receive electrical signals within their tissues. The movement of certain salts (some negatively charged, some positively charged) between cells creates voltage changes and thus a flow of electricity within any living plant.

Botanists have known about electricity in plants for several decades. Now modern equipment enables them to measure fine differences in voltages within plants. Electrodes placed on any two points of a plant—even on opposite sides of a leaf—detect differences in voltage. Any change in a plant's environment—in the amount or quality of light, water, or air—can cause measurable changes in voltage at various places on the plant. Powerful sound waves or an injury also may affect sensitive parts of the plant, altering the electrical voltage.

From measurements of such slight electrical changes, some people were led to claim that plants have feelings. Far from discovering something unknown about plants, however, they had simply detected voltage changes already known to occur routinely. Others claimed that plants responded to human thoughts or prayers. These claims, however, were based on poorly planned "experiments," which led inevitably to untrustworthy results. In fact, a British scientist reportedly duplicated the results of some of these "experiments" by substituting a damp cloth for a living plant. Another scientist said that his measurements of plant voltage levels changed when he wore rubber-soled shoes. Experts in detecting and interpreting electrical activity in plants and animals warn that it is difficult to eliminate the effects of such outside sources.

When people claim that they detect fear, worry, or

other feelings in plants, they reveal more about humans than about the plant kingdom. Many people enjoy attributing human qualities to their pets and plants. Some people talk to their plants and even believe this benefits their growth. Some choose certain kinds of music for the listening pleasure of their plants. Almost every year there are news reports that a student has proved that plants prefer classical music to acid rock—or the other way around. Inquiries always show, however, that the so-called experiment has proved nothing, except perhaps the person's desire for a certain conclusion.

The first known investigator of the possible effects of music on plants was Charles Darwin, who played a bassoon close to a mimosa. He observed no reaction from this plant, which is so sensitive to touch. Nevertheless, scientists with modern, sophisticated equipment have found that plants are indeed affected by sound.

Sound waves transmitted to plants—and to animals—can cause cell contents to vibrate. Carefully designed experiments have shown that sounds of certain frequencies and volume can stimulate growth of wheat plants. Other frequencies and volumes retard growth of coleus plants. But these findings tell us nothing about the effects of different kinds of music on plants. Even the simplest musical composition is quite complex and has many different qualities—various speeds, pitches, and volumes. Plants experience all of these qualities whether they "listen" to Bach or the Beatles. Sound affects plants, but to imagine that plants hear what we hear or that they have musical preferences is wishful thinking.

In 1983, botanists discovered that trees seem capable of sending signals to other plants. A tree attacked by insects increases the production of bad-tasting chemicals in its leaves. Then the odor of these chemicals, or of another substance, passes through the air to nearby trees, which also produce insect repellents. This is an important discovery, but it does not mean that plants communicate as humans do.

As much as we may want plants to be like us, they remain quite different. Botanists have hardly begun to understand many of the chemical complexities of plant life; yet they do know that plants are in some ways much simpler than the simplest insect. Plants are nevertheless remarkably in touch with their environment, sensing it with pigments, statoliths, and other receptors, responding to it with special cells, tissues, and hormones. In both their similarities to animals and their differences from them, plants hold many wonders to discover.

Glossary

Note: Words printed in *italics* are defined within this glossary.

ABSCISIC ACID   a *hormone* produced in plants that usually inhibits growth and *germination* of seeds. It also causes *guard cells* to take up water and swell, thereby closing leaf *stomata.*

ANGIOSPERM   plant that reproduces by means of *flowers* and whose seeds are enclosed in *fruits.*

AUXIN   a growth regulator, or *hormone*, that stimulates cell elongation and division, promoting growth and development.

CELL   the basic structural unit of plants and animals. A plant cell is surrounded by a nonliving cell wall.

CHLOROPHYLL   a green *pigment* that occurs chiefly in *palisade cells* of leaves, and that is required in the food-making process, *photosynthesis.*

(76)

Glossary

CLONE   a group of organisms descended asexually from a common ancestor.

CONIFER   a tree that bears seeds in cones made of overlapping scales. Coniferous trees, which are *gymnosperms*, include pines, spruces, and firs.

CUTICLE   a waxy substance secreted by *epidermal* cells on their outer walls.

CYTOKININ   a *hormone* produced in plant roots that influences growth and development in other plant parts.

EMBRYO   a young plant in its seed, before the beginning of its rapid growth. Each embryo within its seed has the beginnings of its first leaves, first root, and first bud.

ENDOSPERM   food storage tissue that surrounds the *embryo* plant in a seed of a flowering plant.

EPIDERMAL   having to do with the *epidermis*.

EPIDERMIS   the protective outermost layer of a plant *cell*.

ETHYLENE   a colorless gas that functions as a *hormone* in plants, causing *fruit* to ripen, petals to droop, and leaves to fall.

FERTILIZATION   the fusion of a male sex *cell* with a female sex cell.

FLOWER   the reproductive organ of the *angiosperms*, usually consisting of petals, sepals, *stamens*, and a *pistil*.

FRUIT   a matured *ovary,* or a cluster of matured ovaries, usually containing one or more seeds. In the science of botany, not only apples and bananas but also peas, squashes, peppers, acorns, and grains are all fruits.

GEOTROPISM   plant growth in response to the force of gravity.

GERMINATION   the sprouting or resumption of growth by a seed, spore, or other reproductive structure.

GIBBERELLIN   a substance produced by plants that stimulates stem and root growth, seed *germination*, and flowering.

GUARD CELLS   pairs of *epidermal* cells that enclose and regulate the size of openings called *stomata*.

GYMNOSPERM   a woody, seed-bearing plant whose seeds are not enclosed in *ovaries*. They include the ginkgo, cycads, and such *conifers* as pines and junipers.

HORMONE   a substance produced by living organisms that regulates growth and development.

LIGNIN   a complex compound that is a vital part of wood. Lignins function as binders and supports for the fibers of many plants.

MERISTEM   a plant tissue composed of *cells* that are capable of frequent division. Meristem tissue is found near the tips of roots and stems and, in many plants, as an inner layer (called cambium) along the lengths of roots and stems.

OVARY   the enlarged base of a flower's *pistil* in which *ovules* develop.

OVULE   an immature seed, containing an egg nucleus, that develops after fertilization into a seed containing an *embryo* plant.

PALISADE CELL   a long, cylindrical leaf *cell* that contains *chlorophyll* and in which most food making occurs.

PHLOEM   the plant food-conducting tissue that consists mostly of *sieve tube* cells.

PHOTOSYNTHESIS   the manufacture of food, mainly sugar,

from carbon dioxide and water in the presence of *chloro-phyll*, using solar energy and releasing oxygen.

PHOTOTROPISM   growth induced by the stimulus of light. It can be either away from light (negative phototropism) or toward light (positive phototropism).

PIGMENT   a substance that produces colors in plant or animal tissues. Plant pigments include *chlorophylls* (greens), anthocyanins (reds, purples, blues), and carotenoids (yellows, oranges, orange-reds).

PISTIL   the central structure of a *flower* that encloses one or more *ovules*.

POLLEN   the male sex *cells* of seed plants.

POLLEN TUBE   an outgrowth of a *pollen* grain carrying male sex *cells* to the egg in the *ovule*.

POLLINATION   in *angiosperms,* the transfer of *pollen* from a *stamen* to a *stigma*.

RESPIRATION   the chemical process by which organic material is broken down, releasing energy.

RHIZOME   an underground stem that grows horizontally and is often enlarged with stored food.

SIEVE TUBE   a series of sievelike *cells* joined end to end; they are passageways for food, in the form of sugary sap.

SKOTOTROPISM   growth toward darkness.

STAMEN   the *pollen*-producing structure of a *flower.*

STATOLITH   a movable starch grain that occurs in some plant *cells* and that moves in response to gravity, stimulating vertical growth when a plant part is tipped from its normal position.

STIGMA the part of a flower's *pistil,* usually located at its top, upon which *pollen* must be deposited for *pollination* to occur.

STOMA (pl. stomata) an opening between two *guard cells* in the *epidermis* of a plant. Guard cells regulate the size of stomata, which are passageways for the exchange of gases between plants and the atmosphere.

TENDRIL a slender, coiling structure that aids the support of plant stems; it is usually a modified stem or leaf.

TRACHEID CELL an elongated *cell* with thick, pitted walls through which water and minerals are conducted.

TRANSPIRATION the emission of water vapor from plants, chiefly from leaf *stomata.*

TROPISM a growth response resulting from an external stimulus, such as light, darkness, gravity, or touch.

TURGOR PRESSURE the pressure that develops in a *cell* as a result of the uptake of water; the pressure is exerted against the cell wall.

VACUOLE a space within a *cell,* enclosed by a membrane, and containing a water solution of sugars and other substances.

VEGETATIVE REPRODUCTION plant reproduction by a vegetative part of a plant—such as a leaf, root, or stem cutting—that does not involve fusion of sex cells.

VESSEL CELLS elongated *cells* that are joined end to end, forming hollow tubes that conduct water and minerals.

XYLEM a complex plant tissue, composed of such *cells* as *tracheid, vessel,* and ray cells, and wood fibers, which functions mainly to conduct water and minerals.

(80)

Further Reading

Alexander, Taylor R., *et al. Botany: A Golden Science Guide.* Racine, Wisc.: Western Publishing Company, Inc., 1970.

Allan, Mea. *Darwin and His Flowers: The Key to Natural Selection.* New York: Taplinger Publishing Co., Inc., 1977.

Cook, Robert. "Attractions of the Flesh." *Natural History,* January 1982, pp. 21–24.

———. "Long-lived Seeds." *Natural History,* February 1979, pp. 55–60.

———. "Plant Parenthood." *Natural History,* July 1981, pp. 30–35.

———. "Reproduction by Duplication." *Natural History,* March 1980, pp. 88–93.

Duddington, C. L. *Evolution and Design in the Plant Kingdom.* New York: Thomas Y. Crowell Company, 1969.

Galston, Arthur. *Green Wisdom: The Inside Story of Plant Life.* New York: Basic Books, Inc., Publishers, 1981.

———. "The Unscientific Method." *Natural History*, March 1974, pp. 18–24.

Galston, Arthur, Peter Davies, and Ruth Sattler. *The Life of the Green Plant*, 3rd ed. Englewood Cliffs, N.J.: Prentice-Hall, Inc., 1980.

Grossman, Mary Louise. "Ours Was a World Without Flowers Until 'Just Recently.' " *Smithsonian*, February 1979, pp. 119–30.

Gould, Steven Jay. "The Five Kingdoms." *Natural History*, June–July 1976, pp. 30–37.

Klein, Richard. *The Green World: An Introduction to Plants and People*. New York: Harper & Row, Publishers, 1978.

Knutson, Roger. "Flowers That Make Heat While the Sun Shines." *Natural History*, October 1981, pp. 75–81.

———. "Plants in Heat." *Natural History*, March 1979, pp. 42–47.

Meidner, H., and D. W. Sheriff. *Water and Plants*. New York: John Wiley & Sons, Inc., 1976.

Mulcahy, David. "Rise of the Angiosperms." *Natural History*, September 1981, pp. 30–36.

Ray, Thomas, Jr. "Slow-Motion World of Plant 'Behavior' Visible in Rain Forest." *Smithsonian*, March 1979, pp. 121–30.

Regal, Philip. "Ecology and Evolution of Flowering Plant Dominance." *Science*, May 6, 1977, pp. 622–29.

Stone, Doris. *The Lives of Plants: Exploring the Wonders of Botany*. New York: Charles Scribner's Sons, 1983.

Temple, Stanley. "Plant-Animal Mutualism: Coevolution With

Dodo Leads to Near Extinction of Plant." *Science*, August 26, 1977, pp. 885–86.

Torrey, J.G., and D. T. Clarkson, eds. *The Development and Function of Roots*. New York: Academic Press, Inc., 1975.

Walker, Dan. "Plants in the Hostile Atmosphere." *Natural History*, June–July 1978, pp. 75–81.

Wareing, P. F., and Phillips, I.D.J. *The Control of Growth and Differentiation in Plants*. Elmsford, N.Y.: Pergamon Press, Inc., 1978.

Went, Frits. *The Plants* (Life Nature Library). New York: Time-Life Books, a Division of Time Inc., 1963.

Zimmermann, Martin. "Piping Water to the Treetops." *Natural History*, July 1982, pp. 6–13.

Index